Dear Child of Mine,

*I cherish you so much
I gave my own Son to make you
Mine, give you everlasting life, shower
you with favor, answer your prayers,
help you rest in Me and
show you My love every day.
John 3.16*

Love Letter from God

This is a work of non- fiction.

Text and Illustrations copyrighted

by A 2 Z Press LLC ©2023

All rights reserved. No part of this book may be

reproduced, transmitted, or stored in an information retrieval

system in any form or by any means,

graphic, electronic, or mechanical without prior written

permission from the publisher.

Printed in the United States of America

A 2 Z Press LLC

PO Box 582

Deleon Springs, FL 32130

bestlittleonlinebookstore.com

sizemore3630@aol.com

440-241-3126

ISBN: 978-1-946908-65-0

Dedication

To My dear child,
Love, God

*More than anything in the world, I want you to know that I love you with an everlasting love - a love that makes **you** the focus of all My attention. Your heart and you are My most precious possessions. Jeremiah 31.3.*

I know that the deep, deep, very deep need of your heart is to feel loved. I know you have struggled with feeling unloved often in your life. I want you to know My love.

Today, google the song, 'The Steadfast Love of the Lord Never Ceases' and bask in its truth.
Lamentations 3.22-23

I call you My friend... John 15.15. Friend is a word to mean we are close to each other and share everything... that we share a bond of mutual affection... we know each other... we enjoy each other ...relationship ... friends.

Today, Please google the fun song, 'Friend Like You,' by Geaff Moore and know I need you and love you.

You have never been out of My care. I am the God Who sees you! I see every moment of every day, every tear, every happy moment when you accomplish something meaningful to you, every moment you feel unseen, every struggle, I see you...Genesis 16.13.

*Today, please google 'His Eyes'
by Steven Curtis Chapman*

I made you and knew you before you were ever born. I know every thought you think and words you want to say. You are wonderfully made - I love every thing about you. I made your beautiful eyes and your sweet smile, your love for flavored things to drink, all the plans you want to make.....Psalms 139

Today, I want you to google 'Nothing is Beyond You' sung by Amy Grant and remember I am everywhere you are and love everything about you.

…. I made you perfect. You are brilliant…… take time to read about things and understand Me and the world around you……. don't be afraid to learn so many things and make Me proud, I am with you at all times…

Psalms 139

Today, please google 'By Your Side' by Tenth Avenue North

You are creative, so creative, and I am so thrilled with your creativity because I am a creative God and shared My talents with you. Psalms 139

Today, please google 'Take You at Your Word' by Avalon

I want to make you a blessing to all and bless the roads for all the jobs or careers you want to enjoy. I have your days planned for good.. Psalms 139

Today, google 'O Faithful God' and know I am always by you and I dry your eyes, I am a faithful God.

But your talents are not where your true and lasting value are and the reasons I love you. I love you because you are you and you are Mine. I set unbelievable value on your distinctness . When I talk about 'losing yourself' I mean for you to abandon the clamour of self-will - once you do that, I give you back all YOUR personality and boast that when you are wholly Mine, you are more YOURSELF than ever— the you I created to be specially and ONLY you.

I LOVE YOU

DEEPER THAN THE OCEAN

HIGHER THAN THE SKY....

*Today please google 'He Knows My Name'
sung by Don Moen*

My dear child: Fear not, for I have called you by your name; you are Mine - MY VERY OWN. When you see yourself, know I see YOU and love everything about you. Isaiah 43.1.

Today I want you to google 'Our Father' by Don Moen

Because of My great love your you, I pray for you at all times. I pray for you to know Me more, see My favor each day, succeed, rest in Me, believe I love you, and more.... Hebrews 7.25

Please google 'Adonai' by Avalon

One of the prayers I pray for you is: ... 'because I have heard of your faith in Me, ... I do not cease to give thanks for you, I always pray ... to grant you a spirit of wisdom and revelation of insight into mysteries and secrets in the deep and intimate knowledge of Me. I pray that by having the eyes of your heart flooded with light, you can know and understand the hope to which I have called you, and how rich is My glorious inheritance in the saints, My set-apart ones, And so that you can know and understand what is the immeasurable and unlimited and surpassing greatness of My power in and for you who believe, as demonstrated in the working of My mighty strength, - that you can really see the real Me and believe I love you....
Ephesians 1.15-19

Please google 'Lord Let Your Glory Fall' by Matt Redman

….and another prayer I pray for you is 'I want to grant you out of the rich treasury of My glory to be strengthened and reinforced with mighty power in the inner man by the Holy Spirit, Himself, indwelling your innermost being and personality. May I, Christ, through your faith actually dwell, settle down, abide, make My permanent home in your heart! May you be rooted deep in love and founded securely on love, that you may have the power and be strong to apprehend and grasp with all the saints, My devoted people, the experience of that love, what is the breadth and length and height and depth of it; That you may really come to know practically, through experience for yourselves My love which far surpasses mere knowledge without experience; that you may be filled through all your being unto all the fullness of God may have the richest measure of the divine Presence, and become a body wholly filled and flooded with God Himself!
Ephesians 3.16-19

Please google, 'Say the Name' by Margaret Becker

I pray that you see and experience how I am able to do immeasurably more than all you ask or imagine, according to My power that is at work within you.... Ephesians 3.14-21 My blessings to you are pressed down, shaken together, and running over! Luke 8.38

Please google 'Jubilate' by Babbie Mason and dance for JOY that I really love you and take care of you.

Lift up your eyes ...and see! Who has created these? I am He Who brings out their host by number and calls them all by name; through the greatness of My might and because I am strong in power, not one is missing or lacks anything. Do you think your way and lot are hidden from Me? Do you think I passed over you without regard? Have you not heard that I do faint or grow weary... I give power to the faint and weary, and to him who has no might I increase strength causing it to multiply and making it to abound. Isaiah 40. 26-29

Please google 'Lord I Lift Your Name on High'

I have been young and now am old and have not seen the righteous forsaken or their seed begging bread and YOU will never be denied what you need and want. I care for everything about you... Psalm 37.25. The Earth and its fullness are Mine ... Psalm 24.1

*Today please google, "His Eye is on the Sparrow'
by Larnelle Harris*

I want you to know that I shed light on you and your pathway, My uncompromisingly righteous. I want you to experience the irrepressible joy which comes from consciousness of My favor and protection. I am with you and support you whatever path you take... Psalm 97.11

Please google 'Who You Say I Am' by Hillsong Worship

I want you to know that I am touched with everything that hurts you and causes you to struggle or not be able to cope... so boldly come to Me with everything. Hebrews 4.15 - 16 I know a merry heart is good medicine, but a wounded spirit - who can bear that? I want to heal you because I know any wounds you may have. Proverbs 17.22

Today I want you to google two songs
'Maker of My Heart' by Glad and
'Mercy for the Memories' by Goeff Moore

I, the Lord, am your Shepherd - to feed, guide, and shield you, My child, and you shall not lack. Psalm 23.1

Today I want you to google "Come, Let us Worship and Bow Down' by Courthouse Road Church

I make you lie down in fresh, tender green pastures; I always lead you beside the still and restful waters.
Psalm 23.2

*Today please google 'Place in This World'
by Michael W Smith*

I want to refresh and restore your life, your self; I lead you in the paths of righteousness uprightness and right standing with Me - not for your earning it, but for My Name's sake. Psalm 23.3

Today please google 'Pierce My Ear Oh Lord My God'

Yes, even if, you walk through the deep, sunless valley of the shadow of death, I don't want you to fear or dread any evil, for I am with you; My rod is to protect and My staff to guide and I will comfort you.
Psalm 23.4

Today I want you to google 'He is Yahweh'

I prepare a table before you in the presence of all your enemies. I anoint your head with oil; and I want your brimming cup to always run over with knowing that I love you and care for you and protect you. No one can hurt you. Psalm 23.5

Today I want you to google 'Fill My Cup' by Andrew Ripp

Surely, and, or, only goodness, mercy, and unfailing love shall follow you all the days of your life, and through the length of your days My house and My presence shall be your dwelling place. Psalm 23.6

Today I want you to google 'Better is One Day,'

I want you to know that nothing and no one can ever separate you from Me and My love. Romans 8.38-39 because My everlasting arms are under you at all times. Deuteronomy 33.27

Today please google, "No One Loves Me Like You' by Jars of Clay

I don't want you to fret or be anxious for anything, bring everything to Me, just praise Me and tell Me everything. Write notes to Me, sing to Me... Philippians 4.6

Today please google 'You Are Faithful' by Billy and Sarah Gaines

You will no longer be termed 'forsaken,' nor will your land be called 'desolate' any more. But you will be called Hephzibah, My delight is in her, and your land be called Beulah [married]; for I, the Lord, delight in you, and your land shall be protected by Me, the Lord. I, your God, will rejoice over you. Isaiah 62.4-5

*Today I want you to google 'Sing Over Me'
by the Second Chapter of Acts*

You will also be so beautiful and prosperous as to be thought of as a crown of glory and honor in My hand, and a royal diadem, exceedingly beautiful in My hand. Isaiah 62.3 YOU ARE A PRINCE OR PRINCESS EVEN WHEN YOU DON'T FEEL LIKE ONE!

Today I want you to google, 'We Fall Down, We Cast Our Crowns,' by Maranatha Music

For the Spirit which you have now received is not a spirit of slavery to put you once more in bondage to fear, but you have received the Spirit of adoption, the Spirit producing sonship in the bliss of which we cry, Abba - Father! Romans 8.15 I am Dad, your Abba - Daddy - amid all the chaos of your heart and mind. Now and always.

Please google 'Scars in Heaven' by Casting Crowns

I open My hand and satisfy every living thing with favor. This means you, too, My child, in your pursuit of happiness, I lead the way. Psalm 145.16

Please google 'Bless the Broken Road' by Selah

Remember, though the mountains should depart and the hills be shaken or removed, yet My love and kindness shall not depart from you, nor shall My covenant of peace and completeness be removed, says I, the Lord, Who has compassion on you, My child. Isaiah 54.10

Today please google 'The God You Are' by Josh Baldwin

I, the Lord, am a shield for you, your glory, and the lifter of your head. Psalm 3.3 You were never meant to walk this life out in your own strength, I am not only a shield about you, I am your strength.

Today, I want you to google 'A Shield About Me'

I, the Lord, want to be close to you, My child., I want a deeper and deeper walk with you. I want to talk to you and reveal all the deep things of Me. I want you feel Me close every day in every way. 1 Corinthians 2.10

Please google, 'In His Sanctuary' sung by Steve Darmody

Do not fear; for I am with you; do not be dismayed; for I am your God: I will strengthen you; yea, I will help you; yea, I will uphold you with the right hand of My righteousness. Isaiah 41.10. I promise.

Today please google 'Oh for a Thousand Tongues' sung by the 2nd chapter of Acts

I am faithful to you, you can count on Me as I said in My Word. Deuteronomy 7.9 Even if you feel you do not have faith or enough faith, it matters not, I will always be faithful to you. 2 Timothy 2.13

Today, please google 'You are Faithful' by Billy and Sarah Gaines

I want you to know that I think about so, so many times each day that if I could count the number of My thoughts, they would be more in number than the sand. When you awake, even if I could count to the end, I will still be with you and thinking of you, My precious child. Psalm 139.18

Please google 'Word of God Speak' by MercyMe for the Word of God is living and active Hebrews 4.12

Behold, I have graven you upon the palms of My hands; your walls are continually before Me. Isaiah 49.16
No one can take you from My hands.

Today I want you to google 'Isn't He' by John Wimber

Don't worry about what you will wear or eat. I am a giving God and My supply is endless. I own all the cattle on a thousand hills. Psalm 50.10. I am your Father and I know you have need of all these things. Matthew 6.25-32

Today please google 'He Giveth More Grace' sung by Don Moen

I know you so well, the hairs on your head are numbered – I know every detail about you and love every detail about you. This is how much I love you and take time to know you and want you to know Me and My heart for you. Matthew 10.30

Please google, 'Born Again' by Third Day

I want to give you the gift of My peace amid any storm or chaos in this life. I give you My peace because I love you as I loved Jesus - I give the peace to pass any understanding. John 16.33 John 15.6 Philippians 4.7 The punishment that was needful for you to have My peace was put on Jesus the day He died for you. Isaiah 53.5

Please google, 'Brighter Days' by Blessing Offor

Love is patient and kind and bears all things and believes all things and hopes all things and endures all things, love never fails and I AM LOVE. 1 Corinthians 13. You do not have to run anywhere to find yourself or Me. I am right here, always. Read all about Me in My Word. You are not alone.

*Please google 'Then Christ Came'
by MercyMe, Phil Wickham*

You are saved by grace, not works, and you NEVER have to measure up. You measure up just fine as the child I created and love beyond measure. Ephesians 2.8

Please google 'Amazing Grace'

You are My star and you are My favorite child of all and even if your strength fails, I will never leave you or forsake you. Psalm 71.9. I will not break a bruised person or quench a person who is just barely hanging on. Isaiah 42.3

Please google 'His Strength is Perfect' by Steven Curtis Chapman

I love you deeply and command a blessing on you, dear child - even life forever more. Now and always. Psalm 133.3 I satisfy…. your necessity and desire at your personal age and situation with good so that your youth, renewed, is like the eagle's - strong, overcoming, soaring! Psalm 103.5. I have plans for all your ages, all the time.

Please google, 'How Deep the Father's Love'

I want you to dwell in My secret place and abide under My shadow. Say of Me, 'He is my refuge and my fortress: my God; in Him will I trust.' I will surely deliver you from the snare of the fowler, and from the noisome pestilence and cover you with My feathers, and under My wings shall you trust: My truth shall be your shield and buckler. No evil will come to you because I give My angels charge over you. When you call on Me, I will answer and honor you. Psalm 91.1-4, 10-11,15

Today, I want you to google 'Our Eyes Are On You' by John W Stevenson and Christ Emmanuel Christian Fellowship Choir

My way in delivering My people was through the sea, and My paths through the great waters, yet My footsteps were not traceable, but were obliterated. Psalms 77.19. I take My children by a way that cannot been seen by them. I am never at a loss for what to do next for you, My child, and I always know the way.

Please google, 'Because He Lives' by Celtic Worship

The great grace of the Lord Jesus Christ, and the love of God, and the communion of the Holy Ghost, be with you always and forever. Amen. I want you to know My love for you, My child. It is never out of your reach.
I Corinthians 13.14

Today, I would like you to google, 'My Redeemer is Faithful and True' by Steven Curtis Chapman

I whisper in your ear, 'This is why they call Me, Emmanuel - God with YOU. I am always and forever with you. Matthew 1.23. I will never leave you or forsake you. You have MY promise on this. Hebrews 13.5.

This is why I was born on Christmas Day. Just for you, My dear child..'   Love, God

*Please google, 'Born on That Day' by Matt Maher
And 'Always' by Chris Tomlin*

www.ingramcontent.com/pod-product-compliance
Lightning Source LLC
Chambersburg PA
CBHW051400110526
44592CB00023B/2901